Contents

Introduction...Page 3

The New Code of Practice...Pages 4–5

Individual Education Plans..Pages 6–9

Support in the Classroom...Pages 10–13

Reading Age Guidelines...Pages 14–17

S.E.N. Pupils and Self-Esteem..Page 18

Classroom Strategies for Teachers...................................Pages 19–21

Classroom Strategies for Pupils......................................Pages 22–23

Planning Units of Work for S.E.N. Pupils.........................Pages 24–27

Worksheets for Less Able Pupils.....................................Pages 28–29

Identifying Pupils with Specific Learning Difficulties.......Pages 30–31

Supporting Pupils with Specific Learning Difficulties.......Pages 32–35

Hearing-Impaired Pupils in the Classroom.......................Pages 36–37

Visually-Impaired Pupils in the Classroom.......................Pages 38–39

Useful Addresses/Websites...Page 40

Introduction

Recently there have been important legislative changes in the field of Special Educational Needs that are designed to promote an inclusive education philosophy within all schools.

Both the new SEN Code of Practice (January 2002) and the Disability and Discrimination Code (to be introduced in September 2002) have major implications for the way schools cater for SEN pupils.

Above all, the new legislation has greatly strengthened the right of Special Needs pupils to mainstream provision within the education system.

All staff must now take a major responsibility for identification of, and the support for, SEN pupils. This means full involvement in the planning and delivery of a curriculum that genuinely offers opportunity and achievement for SEN pupils.

This handbook has been designed to help the ordinary class teacher cope with this new challenge.

It provides information to help teachers with the identification of pupils with special needs. It also looks at some of the ways subject teachers can contribute towards planning for the effective support of SEN pupils. Finally, it provides many practical ideas for assisting SEN pupils in the classroom.

The New Code of Practice for Special Educational Needs 2002

There are changes to the Code of Practice that affect **all teachers.**
The New Code (January 2002) states that:

> *"All teachers are teachers of pupils with special educational*
> *needs. Teaching such pupils is therefore a whole-school*
> *responsibility, requiring a whole-school response."*

The New Code has simplified the management of special needs
within a school. The original five stages have been reduced to
Entitlement, School Action, School Action Plus and then, if
necessary, ***Statutory Assessment.*** The right of SEN pupils to
mainstream provision has been greatly strengthened and both parents
and pupils are expected to participate fully in the process.

Entitlement

- All pupils are entitled to a suitably differentiated curriculum.

School Action

- School Action implies interventions that are **additional** or **different to** the normal school provision for pupils.

- It is important to be aware that this is **over and above** the school's usual differentiated curriculum.

- The triggers for School Action could be the concern of the teacher or others that, despite the pupil receiving differentiated learning opportunities, progress is not satisfactory.

School Action Plus

- School Action Plus implies the involvement of external agencies to further support the pupil.

- The triggers for School Action Plus are decisions made by the SENCO and colleagues, in consultation with parents, following lack of progress in spite of school action.

Statutory Assessment

- The school may request a statutory assessment for a *Statement of Special Educational Need* if it is felt that the help given through School Action and School Action Plus has not been sufficient to enable the pupil to make adequate progress.

General Points

- The views of pupils must now be taken at all stages.

- Parents must be consulted regularly throughout the process.

- Individual Education Plans must be practical and uncomplicated with only three or four achievable targets.

Individual Education Plans

The strategies that are to be employed to enable the special needs pupil to progress are recorded in an I.E.P. (Individual Education Plan). Under the new Code of Practice the design of I.E.P.s is to be streamlined, with greater emphasis on what can be practically achieved.

- I.E.P.s should record only what is **additional** or **different to** the normal differentiated curriculum.

- The I.E.P. should be crisply written and focus on three or four individual targets.

- Targets should relate to key areas which match the pupil's needs. They may be cross-curricular or subject-specific.

- The pupils should be involved both in the process of setting the targets and in the review process.

- The targets should be realistic and achievable within the time span of the I.E.P.

Drawing up an I.E.P.

The I.E.P. is drawn up after consultation between the SENCO, teachers, pupil and parents. The plan should build on the curriculum that the pupil is already following, along with his or her peers. It is important that the plan should be implemented within the classroom and make use of programmes, activities, resources and assessment techniques that are available to the teacher.

The Individual Education Plan should include description of:

- The nature of the pupil's learning difficulties.
- The provision to be made for the pupil's special needs—extra support/activities/resources.
- Targets to be achieved within a given time.
- Monitoring, assessment and review arrangements.

It is essential that the I.E.P. should be realistic and constructed from clear, simple statements. It is important to set only a few attainable targets and give evidence of specific action taken to try to achieve them within the time span of the I.E.P.

Targets should be:

- **U**   Understandable
- **R**   Relevant
- **S**   Specific
- **M**   Measurable
- **A**   Attainable
- **R**   Realistic
- **T**   Timed

Cross Curricular Involvement

Under the new Code of Practice all staff must be aware that teaching SEN pupils is a whole-school responsibility. This responsibility will generally need to be reflected in the construction of the pupil's I.E.P.

For example, for a pupil with literacy difficulties, subject specialists may consider increasing the time in class given over to aspects of literacy by planning supported written assignments and reading episodes for the pupil as part of a module of work.

These cross-curricular modifications may then be supplemented with specific strategies for helping the pupil access text, such as annotated diagrams, clearly labelled illustrations, taped texts, timelines, flow charts etc. Writing can be supported by extra resources, such as writing frames, writing templates with suggested section headings, story maps, keyword lists, the use of a tape recorder in class for recording key points, the use of a word processor for drafting, and so on.

Involvement of the pupil

Pupils should be centrally involved in the I.E.P. planning process. They must be encouraged to articulate their own strengths and weaknesses as well as discussing how to achieve targets.

I.E.P. Reviews

If a pupil does proceed through the stages of School Action and School Action Plus to Statementing, the written I.E.P.s and reviews will be required as evidence, especially for outside agencies or the L.E.A.

The S.E.N. Coordinator should set a review date for the I.E.P. and organise contributions from subject staff, parents and pupil, which need to be recorded in written form.

Using the I.E.P., comments should be made on:

- The progress made in meeting the targets, including deciding which targets, if any, need to be continued onto the next I.E.P.
- New targets for the next plan, if necessary.
- How successful the implementation of the current plan has been, including evaluation such as:

  — Were the targets set too hard/too easy?

  — Were any changes made to agreed strategies?

  — Did the targets have to be broken down into smaller steps?

  — Were the resources made available adequate?

  — Has the plan lead to greater access to the overall curriculum?

Finally, a decision has to be reached about where to go next. It may be that sufficient progress has been made and no new targets are required. It may be that the pupil has made progress in some areas but further targets are needed in others. It may be that the pupil has made little progress, and so further action, which may include moving on a stage, may be necessary. This decision will be reached by the SENCO, after receiving all the subject reviews, in consultation with the parents and pupil.

Support in the classroom

A learning support assistant in the classroom can offer support in a number of ways:

Supporting the pupils

- By developing an understanding of the specific needs of S.E.N. pupils

- By establishing a supportive relationship with pupils and developing methods of promoting and reinforcing their self-esteem

- By helping pupils to learn as effectively as possible in both group situations and on their own by:
  — clarifying and explaining instructions

  — ensuring pupils are able to use the materials and equipment provided

— motivating and encouraging pupils when necessary

— assisting them in weak areas such as *language, behaviour, reading, spelling, handwriting, presentation, etc.*

— helping pupils to stay on task and finish work set

Supporting the Teacher

- By providing regular feedback about pupils to the class teacher and SENCO

- By liaising with the class teacher to devise differentiated learning activities

- By contributing to the maintenance of pupils' records

Supporting the School

- By contributing to established links between home and school

- By liaising with other members of the team supporting SEN pupils

- By attending relevant in-service training

- By being aware of established school procedures

A Learning Support Contract

In order that the Class Teacher and Learning Support Assistant can be clear about their roles within the classroom, it is often useful to draw up a simple contract that is acceptable to both.

An example of such a contract is shown on the next page. It should be drawn up as follows after negotiation:

The Class Teacher

This section should outline the responsibilities of the Class Teacher, not only to the SEN pupils but also to the Learning Support Assistant. It should contain information such as:

- The teaching/learning materials provided for both the SEN pupils and the Learning Support Assistant.

- The information that the Learning Support Assistant will need from previous lessons in order to establish a pupil's level of work.

- The role of the class teacher with regard to discipline.

- Information about liaison time both before and after the lesson.

- Any other information deemed necessary.

The Learning Support Assistant

This section should outline the responsibilities of the Learning Support Assistant with particular reference to:

- Whether the Learning Support Assistant will work only with identified SEN pupils or also with other pupils in the class.

- How the Learning Support Assistant will work with identified pupils—assist with note taking, support completion of the task, act as a reader, etc..

- How the Learning Support Assistant will assist the teacher.

Learning Support Contract

Class Teacher: Mr J. Bloggs

Support Assistant: Mrs S. Shaw

Subject: Science

Term: Autumn   **Day:** Friday   **Period:** 4

Pupils identified: Wayne Jones, Lee Greenwood, Anthony Hill
Asif Khan, Sally Clark, Mandy Thraves

Class Teacher's Role

- *To enable L.S.A. to carry out their role as described below.*
- *To ensure the L.S.A. is aware of the objectives of each lesson.*
- *To ensure that pupils treat the L.S.A. in an appropriate manner.*
- *To provide the necessary materials and resources so that the L.S.A. can support the pupils effectively.*
- *To liaise regularly with the L.S.A. to discuss the progress of each pupil and consider appropriate means of support.*
- *To support the L.S.A. in the classroom by showing they are a valued member of staff.*

Support Assistant's Role:

- *To advise the teacher on the needs and requirements of identified SEN pupils.*
- *To work with the identified SEN pupils to help them access the curriculum.*
- *To assist the teacher with the preparation of suitably differentiated materials to cater for the needs of the SEN pupils.*
- *To liaise regularly with the teacher to discuss the progress of the SEN pupils in the class.*

Review Date:_____

Signed: Class Teacher:_____ Date:_____

          Support Assistant:_____ Date:_____

Reading Age Guidelines—
Teacher Expectations

RA 10+

The pupil is able to read competently and will improve autonomously given good reading habits...

It is important that the class teacher does not assume that all pupils can cope with text-based work without further help.

Reading Ages give useful information about the pupil's ability to handle text in different contexts. The following guidelines give a general indication of how a pupil's reading age will affect their ability to cope.

Pupils with a reading age of 6+

These pupils should be considered to be *non-readers* (although the teacher should **never say this!**). These pupils cannot deal with text based work without help.

Pupils with a reading age of 7+

These pupils will have some sight vocabulary of common words and will be able to work out phonetically regular words, e.g. *h-a-t, r-u-n*. These pupils will need help with compound words, e.g. *football*.

Pupils with a reading age of 8+

These pupils will probably be able to read most non subject-specific words in a sentence but will need help with subject-specific words and polysyllabic words.

Pupils with a reading age of 9+

These pupils may still make mistakes and be hesitant with reading substantial sections of text. They may be worried about reading aloud, so it is important that the teacher does not insist they do so.

Pupils with a reading age of 10+

These pupils should be able to read competently and will improve autonomously given good reading habits.

Reading Age Guidelines—
Practical Activities for Pupils

Pupils with a reading age of 6+

- Picture sequencing
- Colouring
- Labelling
- Matching
- Tape recording discussions

These pupils should be encouraged to show successfully completed work to other members of staff and be given much praise.

Pupils with a reading age of 7+

- Cloze exercises (filling in missing words)
- Choosing the correct phrase to complete a sentence
- Sentence sequencing (e.g., an L.S.A. can type or write out what a pupil has dictated, cut it into words or sentences and have the pupil arrange it)

Pupils with a reading age of 8+

- Encourage independent writing in response to questions.
- Make key word lists available for topic work to help with spelling.

Pupils with a reading age of 9+

- Encourage independent writing.
- Encourage pupils to look on their own for mistakes (rather than having them pointed out immediately).
- Support the pupil's own correction and redrafting.

Pupils with a reading age of 10+

- Encourage and support independent writing by providing keyword lists for subject-specific words/language.

All pupils

- All pupils benefit from encouragement rather than criticism.
- **Do not** point out mistakes, faults, inadequacies in front of other pupils.

S.E.N. Pupils and Self-Esteem

S.E.N. pupils often have low self-esteem. They can be caught up in a negative cycle which reinforces their lack of success.

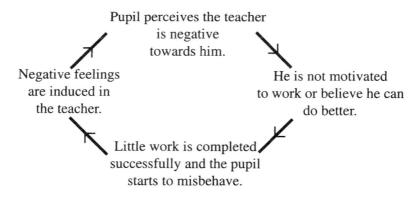

Pupil perceives the teacher is negative towards him.

He is not motivated to work or believe he can do better.

Little work is completed successfully and the pupil starts to misbehave.

Negative feelings are induced in the teacher.

In order to break this cycle it is important for the teacher to deal positively with the pupil's special needs. This involves being aware of the areas of difficulty and adopting strategies which can help. It also involves being patient and prepared to constantly review the strategies employed.

Classroom strategies for teachers

There are a number of simple strategies that the teacher can employ to improve access for SEN pupils in most areas of the curriculum.

Strategies for helping with reading

- Use differentiated text.
- Use larger print.
- Provide pictorial clues to text.
- Present an overview of material to provide cues for the text.
- Identify key points in the text.
- Provide some guidance on best way to approach the text.
- Provide a glossary of any new or difficult words.
- Ask pupils to predict what is in the text.
- Create time for one to one reading with the teacher or L.S.A. .

Strategies for helping with spelling

- Provide a common, everyday word list.
- Provide a subject-specific word list.
- Write important spellings on the board.
- Identify keywords for the lesson.
- Use the *Look-Cover-Write-Check* method for teaching spellings.
- Give spelling tests for keywords.

Strategies for helping with writing and presentation

- Use writing frames to encourage the progressive development of writing skills.
- Correct work for the accurate use of full stops/capital letters.
- Correct work for basic spelling errors.
- Correct work for basic grammar errors.
- Allow pupils time to redraft corrected work.
- Insist on neat corrections when redrafting.
- Insist on use of a ruler for headings.
- Insist on writing on the line.

Strategies for improving behaviour in the classroom

- Make ground rules for the classroom very clear.
- Use humour to encourage good teacher-pupil relationships.
- Use praise regularly.
- Take a genuine interest in what the pupil is doing.
- Reward pupils for completing work successfully—praise, encouragement, achievement stickers, merits, certificates, etc.

- Use appropriate and consistent responses to discipline situations.

- Avoid confrontation over minor discipline problems.

- Signal interference, like a disapproving gesture or expression, may deal with some situations.

- Remain close to pupils whose behaviour is inappropriate.

- Step in early to prevent situations getting out of hand.

- Move pupils around in the class to avoid problems.

- Allowing difficult pupils to take 'time out' can sometimes avert confrontation.

- Appealing to a pupil's sense of co-operation can sometimes be enough to ensure compliance.

- Be consistent and fair with punishments.

- For punishment, take away something the pupil wants:
  — The right to sit where he wants in the class
  — Free time
  — A favoured activity
  — A place in a school team or on a school trip
  — Any privileges available to him.

- Alternatively, give him something he doesn't want:
  — Detention—individual, subject or school.
  — Classroom chores.
  — Negative comments on report.
  — Referral to Head of Year or Headteacher.

Classroom strategies for pupils

SEN pupils should be encouraged to use the following strategies to help themselves work more effectively in the classroom situation.

Strategies for working effectively

- Ask for more explanation from the teacher, if necessary.
- Listen carefully and focus attention on what the teacher says.
- Make an effort to stay on task until the work is complete.
- Sit near the front.
- Select appropriate peers to work with.
- Sit on your own if you are distracted by others.
- Respond positively when help is offered.
- Self evaluate. Ask: is this my best work?
- Use organisational tools available—homework diary, planner, etc.
- Pay attention to comments made on your work.

Strategies for appropriate personal and social behaviour

- Remember instructions from the teacher.
- Avoid distractions—talking, dreaming, etc.
- Think before speaking.
- Avoid aggressive responses.
- Be prepared to discuss problems.
- Be prepared to speak to the Pastoral Team.
- If you are reprimanded, remember it will be because you have done something wrong.
- Accept the consequences of your actions.
- Learn to control anger, count to ten, be prepared to walk away.

Strategies for organisation

- Use an equipment checklist to make sure you have what you need for each lesson.
- Pack your bag for school on the night before.
- Check your timetable for the next day and come to school prepared.

Strategies for improving classwork

- Use a ruler to underline headings.
- Use the correct grip for a pen/pencil; work on letter shape/size.
- Use a dictionary/thesaurus/spellchecker to help with writing.
- With reading and spelling, be aware of chunking into syllables, rhyme patterns, spelling rules and exceptions, etc.
- Use *Look-Say-Cover-Write-Check* for learning new spellings.
- Use keyword checklists to help in subject lessons.

Planning Units of Work for SEN pupils

Be clear about what you are trying to do

- Are the learning outcomes clearly identified?

- Can they be used as a checklist to monitor pupil performance?

- Does the unit clearly identify what *must* be learnt, what *should* be learnt and what *could* be learnt?

- Is there a sufficient range of learning targets to meet the needs of the full range of abilities.

Recognise the pupils' level of understanding

- Is the material relevant to the pupil's current needs?

- Are the central concepts and skills broken down into a hierarchy of development?

- Does each new step build on the previous steps?

Make sure pupils know what is expected of them

- Does the unit have a clearly stated 'end product' which can be either exhibited, demonstrated, explained or summarised in diagrammatic form?

- Is there progression within the unit, and can this be easily recognised by pupils?

- Is there regular feedback for pupils to denote their key achievements within the unit?

Decide how pupil progress will be recorded

- Is there sufficient opportunity for the pupil to demonstrate incidental learning or evidence of prior knowledge and skills?

- Is work only to be presented in written form or has consideration been given to alternative ways of presenting the end product?

- What forms of 'on the spot' assessment and recording does the unit allow/encourage?

- Is the method of assessment clearly stated?

- Does the method of assessment include elements of diagnosis and can these be easily recorded and used for future planning?

- Does the method of assessment match up with the course content?

Consider possibilities for negotiated learning

- Do opportunities exist for pupils to pursue their own interests within the boundaries of the unit subject matter?

- Does the way the unit is planned allow for negotiated targets?

- Can the pupil participate in self-assessment activities as part of the overall assessment process?

Encourage pupils to learn together

- Does the structure of the unit allow for 'mixed skills' groupings, so that pupils can help each other? For example, is there provision for a good reader, a good illustrator, a good discussion leader in each group?

- Is it possible to spend time working in pairs to encourage a 'helper' role?

- Do planned activities within the unit demand co-operation between pupils?

Pay attention to lesson 'rhythms'

- Do the lessons within the unit offer sufficient variety of format?

- Is there a sufficient number of open-ended tasks to allow pupils to work at their own pace?

- Is there a good balance between talking, writing, listening, problem-solving and discussing within the unit?

- Are there opportunities for 'hands on' experiences and multisensory approaches within the unit?

- Do the lessons have a clear format? For example:
  — Pre-lesson preparation
  — A blackboard summary
  — Key points and key words
  —Well established routines for lesson follow-on
  — Clear, reinforced instructions

Respond to individual differences

- Is it possible within the unit to reduce the volume and complexity of the content, while still reaching the main objectives?

- Does the unit make provision for extension work for the more able?

- Are oral and written questions sufficiently varied to take account of different capabilities?

- Is it possible to expand the background material so that the pupils have a greater basis for understanding?

- Does the material to be used include concrete examples as well abstract concepts?

- Are there activities included that allow pupils who are weak readers to contribute positively?

- Does the plan identify the key points of each lesson so that they can be written up on the blackboard or OHP?

- Are there enough examples drawn from real life to illustrate the concepts being taught?

- Has the reading material been differentiated so that less able pupils can access it?

Worksheets for less able pupils

Worksheets for less able pupils need to be written carefully with attention to clear, uncluttered presentation. Some points to bear in mind are:

- Build on the pupil's existing knowledge when introducing new concepts. Don't use new terms without explaining them. For example, for the concept of *authority* start with *parents, teachers, bosses in Saturday jobs,* etc.

- Try to relate assignments to the pupil's personal experience where possible. For example, *Conduct a survey of any pollution you see on your way home.*

- Tasks should be self-contained and all the information needed to complete them readily accessible.

- Repeat tasks in different formats for reinforcement. Slow learners are apt to forget, so once is not usually enough for something to be learned.

- Learning sequences should be broken down into small steps.

- Keep the filling in of missing words exercises to a minimum. Pupils learn more if they have to write out complete sentences. Slow learners need to be able to successfully complete worksheets at the highest level they are capable of.

- When presenting areas of text in a worksheet, use plenty of line spacing (leading), a serif font like Times Roman or Sassoon Primary and a reasonable point size (14 or 16) so that the text is very clear and readable. Nine or ten words per line is good.

- If you can count more than five difficult words in each sentence (Five finger rule) a pupil with a low reading age will probably have great problems coping with the text.

- If there are large areas of text included, leave it left aligned, rather than justified, to avoid the *'rivers of white space'* effect resulting from the irregular word spacing. This effect can cause problems for those whose vision is not very stable.

- In general, avoid using words printed in capital letters as they are harder to read than lower case.

- Keep headings and sub-headings consistent in presentation (size, bold, italic, underline, etc.) throughout the worksheet.

- Keep sub-headings to a minimum, as too many can be confusing.

- Illustrations should be clear and accompanied by captions.

- Try to use the same graphic symbols and effects (arrows, bullet points, etc.) as other school departments to avoid confusion.

- Lots of boxes and arrows may look good but they can make the overall layout of worksheets confusing.

- With maps, make sure they are clear and large enough to work with. If possible, shade areas of sea, as less able pupils often find it difficult to discriminate between land and sea. Be consistent with labelling (always to the right or left of dots, for example).

Identifying pupils with specific learning difficulties (Dyslexia)

Some signs which indicate that pupils make have specific learning difficulties are:

- The pupil seems much brighter than their reading or written work suggests.

- The pupil makes reading errors—guesses at words, omits words, misreads words, mispronounces words, hesitates, reads slowly.

- Punctuation is seldom used. Capital letters are in the wrong place.

- Poor understanding of tense, pronouns and syntax are generally shown.

- There is reversal of numbers (e.g. writing 24 for 42), poor understanding of mathematical language, difficulty with tables.

- Poor spatial ability is shown.

- There is poor sound discrimination.

- Poor graphomotor skills are shown.

- There is directional confusion—left/right, up/down, top/bottom.

- There are problems with sequencing—days of the week, months of the year, etc..
- The pupil has a poor short term memory—difficulties with remembering and following instructions.
- There is a family history where others may have similar problems.
- There is left-handedness or ambidexterity in the family.

Some borderline signs which may mask other symptoms are:
- Poor listening skills
- Being badly organised and forgetful
- Having difficulties with copying from the board.
- Poor concentration
- Appearing lazy and disinterested
- Using many and various delaying tactics
- Hyperactivity.
- Emotional disturbance
- Lack of self control
- General clumsiness
- Finding it difficult to find a starting point in a task
- Needing constant reassurance
- Rejection by the age group for no apparent reason

Supporting pupils with specific learning difficulties (Dyslexia)

A good way to start helping dyslexic pupils is to ask them what they find difficult and to work out some practical classroom strategies.

D on't

Y ell

S ir

L earning is

E asier with

X tra

I nput

C onsideration and

S upport

Copying from the Chalkboard

- Sit the pupils close to the board.

- Make sure that the board is clean.

- Mark each line with a coloured dot or write each line in a different colour.

- Allow the dyslexic child extra time to complete the task.

- If there is a lot of information to take down, make a copy for the pupil and allow him or her to highlight important sections.

Instructions

- Instructions for classroom tasks need to be broken down into small, easily remembered pieces of information.

- Repeat instructions and get the pupil to repeat them back to you.

- Encourage pupils to repeat the instructions silently to themselves.

- Minimise the number of key points they have to remember.

- Sequence the instructions clearly and avoid too many words.

- Use visual images to assist recall.

Classroom Aids

- Diary of things to remember

- Notebook for jotting things down as they arise

- Dictaphone/Tape recorder, especially if they find writing difficult

- Computer with spelling and grammar checking facilities

- Maps/diagrams/lists to explain things as well as verbal instructions

Setting the task

- Ask yourself: 'What do I want the pupil to get out of this exercise?' Then proceed to simplify the task.

- When marking, try to focus on content rather than presentation.

- Write down the pupil's tasks for the lesson so they can tick them off as they complete them.

- Make allowances for dyslexic pupils—perhaps by giving them fewer questions to answer.

Organisation

- Encourage the pupil's self-reliance and sense of responsibility.

- The pupil should have a copy of the timetable at home as well as at school, so that they are encouraged to bring the correct equipment each day.

- Encourage pupils to work systematically through the tasks set.

- Limit the amount of equipment you expect pupils to carry.

Spelling

- Consider different ways of dealing with spelling mistakes. Making the pupils rewrite the words may not help. It may be better to focus on a small number of target words.

- Try not to give long lists of mixed words for the pupil to learn each week. Instead, give only a few words or families of words.

- Encourage pupils to be in control of their own work. Get them to proofread their own work, targeting specific weaknesses which might be keywords, punctuation, grammar, etc.

- Encourage pupils to use a dictionary to check words they are unsure of, or if they have used a word processor to use the spellcheck.

General points

- Do not be afraid to make use of modern technology to help alleviate problems for dyslexic children. The use of laptops, P.C.s, word processors and tape recorders can all be of considerable benefit.

- Don't expect dyslexic pupils to read aloud in class unless, of course, they volunteer to do so.

- Constant overlearning is necessary at every stage. Don't assume that a dyslexic pupil will remember what they learned in your lesson last week.

- Try to judge the dyslexic pupil's ability in your subject from their verbal responses as well as from their written work.

- Be patient with the intermittent nature of the pupil's performance and attention.

- Wherever possible, use a multisensory approach to teaching dyslexic pupils.

- **At all times try to respond positively to the work produced.**

Hearing-Impaired Pupils in the Classroom

Preparation

- Find out in advance the communication needs of the pupil. Do they require the use of any special technical aids?

- If they use a hearing aid, make sure they wear it and that it is switched on.

- Allow more time for discussion work . Communication may take longer if the pupil is lip reading.

Speech

- Speak clearly and at a reasonable pace.

- Do not over-enunciate words or speak too loudly. These make lip reading more difficult.

- Ask the pupil if the pace of speech is appropriate.

Visibility

- The hearing-impaired person needs to be able to see your face.

- Don't obstruct your mouth while talking.

- Try not to move about while giving instructions.

Lighting and Background Noise

- Ensure the light is on your face and never from behind you.

- Light reflecting or flashy jewellery can cause distraction and make lip reading more difficult.

- A quiet, calm atmosphere in the room is helpful.

- Rooms with acoustic treatment (carpets, curtains etc.) make it much easier for the hearing aid wearer.

Facial expression

- Make sure the pupil is looking at you before you start speaking, as meaning is often conveyed in the first phrase.

- Try to maintain eye contact with the pupil and use facial expression to assist in conveying the sense of your words.

- Try not to convey any impatience or frustration in your facial expression, as this will be picked up by the pupil.

Content

- Try to keep what you say simple and to the point, avoiding anecdotes and more complex vocabulary.

- Remember, lip reading is an imperfect tool for full understanding, so be prepared to rephrase what you are saying when required.

General

- Be aware that hearing-impaired pupils may be behind with reading, so allow more time and explain unfamiliar words.

- Do not assume that hearing aids completely correct a hearing problem. They help but do not provide perfect hearing.

- Never say 'Oh, don't bother', 'Never mind' or 'It doesn't matter', as this will reinforce feelings of inadequacy in the pupil.

Visually-Impaired Pupils in the Classroom

Visual problems

Visual impairment can be manifested in a variety of ways:

• Restrictions in the overall field of vision

• Difficulties with fixation on words during reading, causing the pupil's eyes to 'bounce' around the page, thus making concentration difficult

• Difficulties with tracking during reading as the eye moves along one line and on to another

• Distortion of what is being seen or perceived

• Problems in maintaining and changing focus at long and short distances

• Distortions in colour perception

• Visual fatigue

Effect on Learning

*   For the visually impaired, not only are class lessons (heavily reliant as they are on visual stimuli) obviously difficult, but incidental learning and the basic knowledge of everyday objects and experiences will also be restricted.

Technology

*   The provision of a laptop computer with the facility for different sizes of print and word processing may be of great benefit to the visually impaired.

*   Specialist software like *TextHelp,* which allows all the text on a screen to be read aloud by a computer voice, is useful.

*   Allowing pupils to use a hand-held tape recorder for making notes or submitting homework can be beneficial.

Light sensitivity

It has been suggested that up to 30% of the population may be light sensitive to some degree. For most, any resulting visual distortion may be only slight and will not unduly affect the input of visual information. For some, however, a number of effects may make reading difficult:

*   Letters appear to be out of focus with blurring at the edges.

*   Letters or words seem to move around the page .

*   The white space between letters and words is uncomfortably bright, making concentration difficult.

Pupils who suffer from any of the problems described should be referred for further investigation. These effects can often be alleviated to some extent by the use of coloured overlays, tinted lenses or other specialist equipment like the Visual Tracking Magnifier or Optim-eyes™ light.

Useful Addresses/Websites

The British Dyslexia Association
91 London Road
Reading
RG1 5AU
Tel: 0118 9668271

The Scottish Dyslexia Association
Unit 3 Stirling Business Centre
WellGreen
Stirling
FK8 2DZ
Tel: 01786446650

The Dyslexia Institute
133 Gresham Road
Staines
Middlesex
TW18 2AJ
Tel: 01784463851

Royal National Institute for the Blind
Education Centre
Garrow House
190 Kensal Road
London
W10 5BT

Research Centre for the Education of the Visually Impaired
School of Education
University of Birmingham
Edgbaston
Birmingham
B15 2TT

Sight Savers International
Grosvenor Hall
Bolnor Road
Haywards Heath
West Sussex
RH16 4BX
Tel: 01444 412424

The British Deaf Association
1–3 Worship Street
London
EC2A 2AB
Tel: 020 75883520

Friends for Young Deaf People
East Court Mansion
College Lane
East Grinstead
West Sussex
RH19 3LT
Tel: 01342300080

National Deaf Children's Society
15 Dufferin Street
London
EC1Y 8UR
Tel: 020 72500123

Websites

www.desktoppublications.co.uk

www.dyslexia.fsworld.co.uk

www.visualdyslexia.com

www.dyslexiabooks.co.uk

www.dyslexi-inst@connect.bt.com

www.dyscalculia.org

www.dyslexiaa2z.com

EMail

info@dyslexiahelp-bda.demon.uk

dyslexia.scotland@dial.pipex.com